Saint Jude the Apostle

Blessed Are the Persecuted

First Century

Born in Galilee

Feast Day: October 28

Patron of Hope and Difficult Causes

"Blessed are they who are persecuted for the sake of righteousness, for theirs is the kingdom of heaven."
Matthew 5:10

Text by Barbara Yoffie

Illustrated by Chris Sharp

Liguori Publications

A Redemptorist Ministry

Dedication

To my family:
my parents Jim and Peg,
my husband Bill,
our son Sam and daughter-in-law Erin,
and our precious grandchildren
Ben, Lucas, and Andrew

To all the children I have had the privilege
of teaching throughout the years.

Imprimi Potest:
Kevin Zubel, CSsR, Provincial
Denver Province, the Redemptorists

Published by Liguori Publications
To order, visit Liguori.org or call 800-325-9521.

ISBN (print): 978-0-7648-2869-0
ISBN (digital): 978-0-7648-7252-5

Liguori Publications, a nonprofit corporation, is an apostolate of the Redemptorists.
To learn more about the Redemptorists, visit Redemptorists.com.

Printed in the United States of America
28 27 26 25 24 / 5 4 3 2 1
First Edition

Dear Parents and Teachers:

Saints and Me! is a six-set series of children's books about saints, including the *Saints of North America*, who served our homeland; *Saints of Christmas*, who teach us to love Jesus; *Saints for Families*, who modeled God's love within and for the domestic Church; *Saints for Communities*, who served Jesus through various roles and professions; and *Saints for Sacraments*, who showed great love for the sacraments.

The eight books in *Saints of the Beatitudes* (a word meaning "a list of blessings from God") introduce nine holy people who exemplify attributes Jesus articulated in his Sermon on the Mount. Faustina Kowalska's diary, *Divine Mercy in My Soul,* read by millions, helped spread God's message of mercy. Patrick, a missionary, brought Christianity to Ireland. Monica prayed her wayward son, Augustine, would return to the faith. He did and was canonized. Katharine Drexel abandoned her comfortable life to become a nun. Carlo Acutis shared his faith and love of the Eucharist through technology. Bernadette Soubirous experienced visions of the Blessed Virgin Mary. Pope John XXIII convoked the Second Vatican Council, hoping to revive the Church. Jude was an apostle of our Lord.

Which saint was captured by pirates and sold into slavery? Name the saints with back-to-back feast days (August 27–28). Who gave $20 million to build churches and schools? Who created a website about eucharistic miracles? Who did Jesus appear and speak to? Who said, "My job is to inform, not to convince"? Who wrote *Peace on Earth* in 1963? Who is the patron of impossible causes? Find out in the *Saints of the Beatitudes* set—part of the *Saints and Me!* series—and help children connect to the lives of the saints.

Introduce your children or students to *Saints and Me!* as they:

—**READ** about the lives of the saints and are inspired by their stories.

—**PRAY** to the saints for their intercession.

—**CELEBRATE** the saints and relate them to their lives.

Free activities for children to use with this book may be downloaded at Liguori.org.

The Beatitudes

Divine blessings Jesus names in his Sermon on the Mount

Matthew 5:3–12

Saints of the Beatitudes

Patrick
Blessed Are the Poor in Spirit (Verse 3)

Monica and Augustine
Blessed Are the Mournful (Verse 4)

Katharine Drexel
Blessed Are the Meek (Verse 5)

Carlo Acutis
Blessed Are the Righteous (Verse 6)

Faustina Kowalska
Blessed Are the Merciful (Verse 7)

Bernadette
Blessed Are the Pure of Heart (Verse 8)

Pope John XXIII
Blessed Are the Peacemakers (Verse 9)

Jude the Apostle
Blessed Are the Persecuted (Verses 10–12)

Jude was chosen by Jesus to be one of his Twelve Apostles. He followed Jesus and learned about the kingdom of God and how to love and respect other people. He preached the Good News and taught many people about Jesus.

Jude and the other apostles were often persecuted, or treated badly, for their strong faith in Jesus.

Jude was also called Thaddeus, or Jude Thaddeus. His name sounds a lot like another apostle, Judas Iscariot. They were two different people. Judas Iscariot turned against Jesus. He helped soldiers arrest Jesus while he was praying in the garden with the other apostles. Jude would not hurt Jesus. He was a kind and loving apostle.

The Twelve Apostles were faithful followers of Jesus. They did everything together and became very good friends. Jesus taught them important lessons about how to treat people. “Help the poor and the sick. Feed hungry people. Treat all people with love and respect,” Jesus told them.

The apostles were with Jesus when he cured sick people, calmed a storm, walked on water, and multiplied bread and fish for people to eat. "Jesus does amazing things. He is truly the Son of God!" they said.

One night, Jesus and the apostles gathered for a special meal. While they were eating, Jesus told them that he would soon return to his Father in heaven. "Jesus, do not leave us," they cried. They were worried and asked him many questions.

"Have faith in me," Jesus answered. The apostles wanted Jesus to stay with them and teach them more about the kingdom of God.

After their meal, Jesus and his friends went to a nearby garden to pray. It was quiet and peaceful there. Jesus walked ahead of them and knelt down to pray. "I am so sleepy," said one of the apostles. Some of the apostles fell asleep on the ground. They woke up suddenly when they heard the shouts of soldiers.

Judas Iscariot was standing next to Jesus when the soldiers grabbed him and took him away. His enemies put him to death on a cross. Jesus' body was placed in a tomb. The apostles were very sad and felt alone. But three days later, Jesus came out of the tomb. Jesus had risen from the dead!

Jesus appeared to his apostles and other followers for several weeks. One special day, he met with the apostles and told them, "Go to towns near and far and teach people about me and God's love. I must return to my Father, but do not worry. I will send the Holy Spirit to help you!" Jesus blessed his friends and was taken to heaven to be with his Father.

The apostles prayed and waited for the Holy Spirit. Then early one morning, something wonderful happened! A strong wind blew, and small flames of fire appeared over each of their heads. "Jesus has sent us the Holy Spirit! It is time to tell everyone the Good News about Jesus."

They were not afraid anymore. Instead, they were filled with wisdom and courage. The apostles traveled from town to town preaching and teaching about Jesus. They had exciting news to share with everyone!

Jude went to Samaria, Syria, Persia, and Mesopotamia. He traveled to many towns and began to preach. He taught people how to pray and told them about the miracles of Jesus.

Jude healed the sick and performed miracles in Jesus' name! Many people believed in other gods. They laughed at Jude and made fun of him. One man grumbled, "I do not believe you and your silly stories about Jesus!"

Being a missionary is hard work. Jude tried his best and never gave up. He spoke to small groups and big crowds. The Holy Spirit was with him every day giving him courage and strength. Soon his preaching began to make a difference.

People started to believe in the good things Jesus had done and they were baptized. His followers, called Christians, formed small churches in different places. This is how the Church began. As the faith spread, the Church grew.

The Apostle Simon met Jude in Persia. Jude was happy to see Simon and welcomed his help. He warned Simon, "Some people are very mean, Simon. We must be careful." Together, they walked from town to town preaching the Good News.

Upon entering one town, they were approached by some angry men. They shouted and made threats to Jude and Simon. "Stop telling people about the man called Jesus. We will put an end to your preaching!" Before they could leave, the men grabbed Jude, then Simon, and killed them. The Church honors Jude and Simon as martyrs.

After his death, Jude's body was placed in a tomb in Saint Peter's Basilica in Rome.

People prayed to Saint Jude and asked him for help. When their prayers were answered, the news spread fast. People told their friends, "Pray to Saint Jude. He will take your prayers to God. Your most impossible prayers will be answered!"

Lots of people pray to Saint Jude when they have a serious problem. Called the patron of hope and impossible causes, he gives hope and peace to anyone who is worried or in trouble. Shrines and churches around the world are named for Saint Jude. He is a very popular saint in the Catholic Church.

In Christian art, Jude is holding a walking stick, because he was a brave missionary. He has a flame over his head, which is the fire of the Holy Spirit, who gave him the courage to do God's work. Jude holds a large medal with a picture of Jesus on it, close to his heart. He loved Jesus very much, and was a faithful apostle and good friend. He shares his message of hope with all of us.

Pray to Saint Jude, he listens and cares.
You can offer him your most serious prayers.

♥ ♥ ♥

Dear Saint Jude,

Your faith in Jesus was very strong.

You were a brave missionary and
preached the Good News of Jesus.

Thank you for giving me hope
when I am worried.

I know God will always help me.

Amen.

GLOSSARY (NEW WORDS)

Apostles: Twelve men chosen by Jesus to preach the Gospel and lead his followers

Courage: Being strong when faced with something that is difficult or painful to do

Good News: The message that Jesus died and rose again so people can be with him in heaven

Holy Spirit: The third person of the Blessed Trinity; he is our helper and guide

Hope: A virtue that helps you look to the future with faith and trust

Kingdom of God: God's love working in the world through his believers

Martyr: Someone who gives up his or her life on behalf of a belief or cause

Miracle: An amazing event that cannot be explained

Missionary: A person who teaches the faith or preaches the Gospel in a certain place

Persecuted: Someone who is treated badly because of what they believe or do

Shrine: A holy place that marks the spot or an event in a saint's life or a miracle

Tomb: A place used for burying someone who has died

saints and me!

SAINTS FOR SACRAMENTS

Booklets in this set were honored by the Association of Catholic Publishers!

John the Baptist:
Saint for Baptism
827969

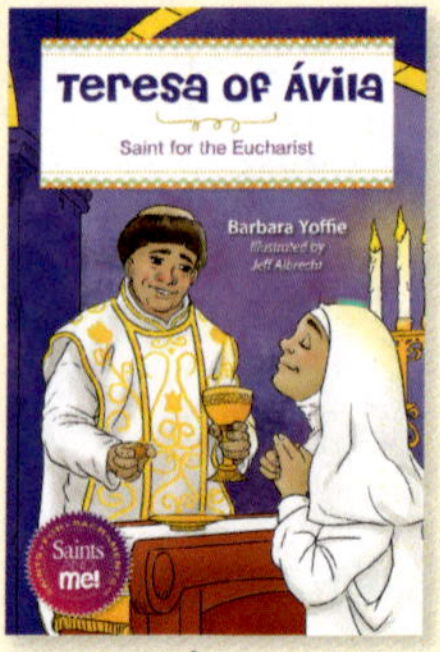

Teresa of Ávila:
Saint for the Eucharist
827938

Padre Pio:
Saint for Reconciliation
827921

Philip Neri:
Saint for Confirmation
827976

Maximilian Kolbe:
Saint for Anointing
of the Sick 827983

Louis and Zélie Martin:
Saints for Matrimony
827945

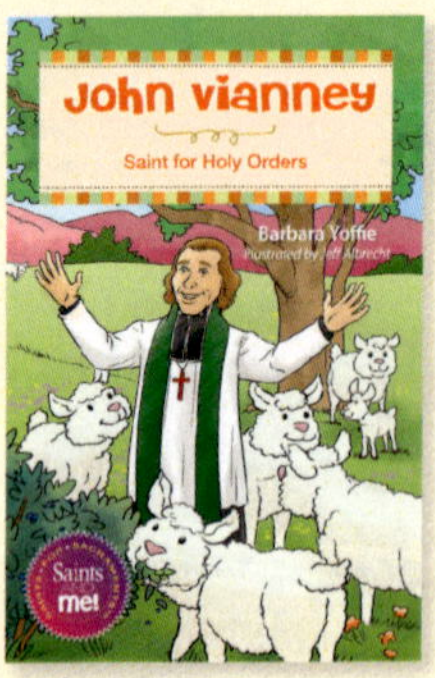

John Vianney:
Saint for Holy Orders
827952

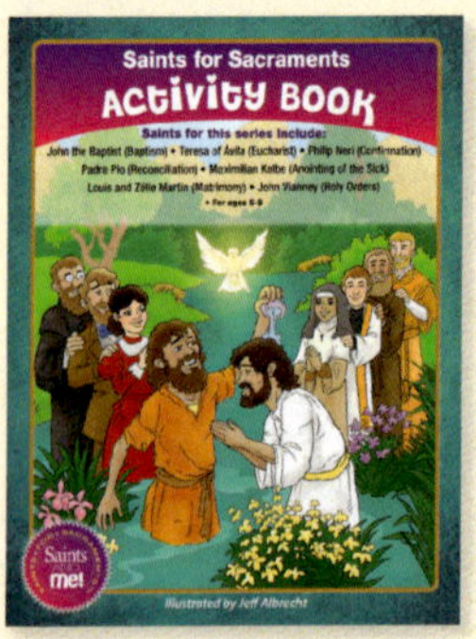

Saints for Sacraments
Activity Book 828010

Get the Complete Set!

Saints for Sacraments
Collection A00085
(*Activity Book* sold separately)

Booklets: 32 pages, 5.5 x 8.5,
Full-color illustrations

Activity Book: 96 pages, 8.5 x 11

Order today! Call 800-325-9521 or visit Liguori.org.